KEN ROBBINS

Fire

THE ELEMENTS

H E N R Y H O L T A N D C O M P A N Y · N E W Y O R K

Henry Holt and Company, Inc.
Publishers since 1866
115 West 18th Street
New York, New York 10011

Henry Holt is a registered
trademark of Henry Holt and Company, Inc.

Published in Canada by Fitzhenry & Whiteside Ltd.,
195 Allstate Parkway, Markham, Ontario L3R 4T8.
Library of Congress Cataloging-in-Publication Data
Robbins, Ken.
Fire / Ken Robbins. (The elements)
Summary: Examines fire in all its forms, from volcanic
flames to forest fires.
1. Fire—Juvenile literature.   2. Combustion—Juvenile literature.
[1. Fire.]   I. Title.   II. Series: Robbins, Ken. Elements.
QD516.R577   1995   541.3'61—dc20   95-25209

ISBN 0-8050-2293-7
First Edition—1996
Printed in the United States of America on acid-free paper. ∞
1   3   5   7   9   10   8   6   4   2

The photographs for this book are hand-colored with water-based dyes.

For Lily Henderson

Anything that's red hot, fierce or angry, burning, warming, incandescent, or transforming; all that's purifying, sterilizing, useful, destructive, consuming, or bright. Anything that produces light and gives us sight. The sun itself, the flames of hell, neon signs of every kind, a burning bush that's not consumed, a fireplace in the living room, a welding torch, a lamp lit on the old front porch; steel mills, lightning, candles, a barbecue grill, the thing that makes the toast turn brown; the terrible sight of a house burned down, the fatal charms of firearms—all these things and more besides are part of what we mean by fire.

MAN WITH TORCH, CAPE COD, MASSACHUSETTS

FIRE

People once believed that the entire world was a mixture of earth, water, air, and fire. In modern times we've come to see that substances like earth and air and water, too, are mixes of different molecules. But fire is different—it isn't really stuff, it's a process, an action, a thing that occurs. Under certain conditions, matter will burn. Fire is really a chemical change. It produces light and gives off heat when molecules are rearranged. The thing that's on fire is called the fuel, and as it burns it combines with oxygen, as a rule; but we use the word "fire" in many ways.

There's nuclear fusion—that's the heat of the sun, or the way that your body "burns up" your food when you run. There's electrical energy, which can produce the awesome and frightening power of lightning. The word "fire" is also often loosely linked with the ways humans feel and think: we speak of a fire in someone's eyes, and the flames of passion that mark desire, a fire in the belly that shows ambition, and there's a spark in the mind of recognition. These are expressions that are used every day, they're not meant in a literal way— they're metaphors and they say a lot about what we mean when we say something's "hot." The fact that we use them is a definite sign of how important fire is in our minds.

FIRE

SUNSET AND SEA STACK, YACHATS, OREGON

THE SUN

HUNTER'S MOON, EAST HAMPTON, NEW YORK

The universe and all the stars began with fire—an immense explosion a long, long, long, long time ago. The sun, of course, is just the closest of the stars you can see, and it's the source of all our energy. Over eighteen thousand degrees centigrade and ninety-three million miles away, it heats the earth and lights up the day. Even the moon, which glows in the night, shines with the sun's reflected light.

THE SUN

PU'O O'O VOLCANO, KILAUEA, HAWAII

VOLCANO

OLD FAITHFUL, YELLOWSTONE NATIONAL PARK, WYOMING

Exactly when the earth was created no one really knows, but there's pretty good evidence that shows that it was probably around four thousand million years ago. Back then it was no more than a chunk of stuff, a fiery accumulation of primitive gases and cosmic dust. The earth has been cooling ever since, yet for five hundred million years it remained too hot for life to exist. Although it's cool enough now, the earth is still molten at its core (five thousand degrees centigrade or more), and once in a while that fire erupts, and liquid rock comes boiling up from the depths of the world, belching smoke and spewing flame. Steaming geysers also show how hot the earth is down below.

VOLCANO

LIGHTNING, GRAND CANYON, ARIZONA

LIGHTNING

Sometimes, when cold air mingles with warm, the result is a violent electrical storm. Electrical fire stabs the air, leaving stark and jagged patterns there for a startled moment and then they're gone, and the thunder rumbles on and on. Most lightning strikes quite harmlessly, but a bolt can shatter a giant tree, electrocute a human being, or start a raging forest fire.

FIRE DAMAGE, YELLOWSTONE NATIONAL PARK, WYOMING

WILDFIRE

WILDFIRE, NEAR POLSON, MONTANA

Grasses and trees, especially when they're dry, are very easily set on fire. A careless camper or a lightning strike in the middle of the night can have a whole region on fire by morning. Trees are destroyed and animals are killed, burned by the fire or choked by the swirling billows of thick black smoke. Fires like that are awesome things with terrible, destructive power—and somewhere on earth, lightning starts one every hour. Recently, though, we've come to see that a natural fire is not all a bad thing. Nature will seize on any excuse to turn a disaster into good use. After a fire is over, burnt out and cold, new plants thrive because the old ones have been cleared away, and there's room for new ones to grow.

WILDFIRE

CONTROLLED BURN, MONTAUK, NEW YORK

C O N T R O L L E D   B U R N

CONTROLLED BURN, SPRINGS, NEW YORK

Considering how dangerous they are, it's a natural impulse to put fires out, but whenever fire changes the land, some things are lost and some are gained. In the past, the native people of the American plains set intentional fires on the great prairies to keep them open and free of trees—so the great herds of bison would have grass for feed, and the Indians could hunt and have enough to eat.

Today we sometimes set fires to adjust the balance of trees and grass and brush. If there's too much of one or else not enough, we set a fire to sustain the ecology that used to be before people were around to interfere. Controlled fires are intentionally set, but the people who light them never let the fire travel or get out of hand. They carefully study the lay of the land; before they set a fire they have to know the speed of the wind and which way it blows, the temperature of the air, the condition of all the trees and grasses there—it has to be done with enormous care.

CONTROLLED BURN

CAMPFIRE, EAST HAMPTON, NEW YORK

CAMPFIRE

CAMPFIRE, EAST HAMPTON, NEW YORK

For a picnic on the beach, or if we're camping at night, we build a fire for warmth and light, the way our ancestors did centuries ago. For them it was more a matter of survival than fun—they had no other source of heat at night, and wild beasts were frightened by the fire. It made them feel safer, in any case, to gather together around a roaring blaze.

CAMPFIRE

LIGHTED MATCH

MAKING A FIRE

FLINT AND STRIKER

In ancient myth, Prometheus gave us fire as a gift, but in reality people probably stole a branch from a burning tree that had been set on fire by a lightning bolt. Perhaps they carried that branch to where they lived, and fed it fuel like leaves and twigs, and made a fire, and learned to control it. More fuel makes a fire grow; less fuel and the fire burns low and then goes out. If someone got careless and the fire died, that was that. No one would have known where or when a lightning bolt would strike again.

Eventually, people learned that if you rub two sticks together long enough, they'll burn. Friction always generates heat. (If you don't believe that, rub your hands together rapidly.) Striking a flint with a piece of steel is another way of making a spark. Today, of course, we can just strike a match, and the friction causes the sulfur at the tip to catch fire.

FRYING EGGS, SUNNY-SIDE UP

COOKING

BACKYARD BARBECUE

Our ancient ancestors ate meat and fruit, berries, nuts, and certain roots. In the beginning they no doubt ate them raw, but sooner or later someone saw that using fire and exposing certain foods to the heat made them easier to eat—tastier, too, and they lasted longer before they spoiled.

Almost every kind of food—burgers, grilled; tomatoes, stewed; baby back ribs, barbecued; potatoes, fried; dumplings, steamed; boiled shrimp; roasted turkey and baked beans; poached eggs and toasted cheese; broiled flank steak—all of these are cooked with flame, or, if not flame, some kind of fire.

COOKING

HEARTH FIRE

HEARTH

Once upon a time, a while ago, a hearth in a home was its heart and soul, a fire for cooking and a source of light and warmth, a place where families would gather in the evening and talk.

These days most of us cook in a kitchen, we have central heat, and when we get together we watch TV, but we still have fireplaces, at least many of us do, and we like to have fires in them, too. They're warm and cozy on a winter's night, and the fire gives off a lovely light.

HEARTH

FOURTH OF JULY, EAST HAMPTON, NEW YORK

FIREWORKS

FOURTH OF JULY, MINOT, NORTH DAKOTA

With bursts of sound and great flashes of light, fireworks are one of the more wonderful sights you'll see on the Fourth of July or any other great anniversary, when people celebrate in a public way whatever it was that happened that day. People gather in a public place as the sun goes down at the end of the day, and when it's finally dark they start the display, and the rockets go off with a boom and a streak of light, and brilliant explosion that lights up the skies—just as in wartime, only nobody dies.

FIREWORKS

STOREFRONTS, SAG HARBOR, NEW YORK

ARTIFICIAL LIGHT

LIGHTHOUSE, MONTAUK, NEW YORK

Long ago, in the dark of night, people weren't able to see very much; they relied on their senses of hearing and touch. Until they learned how to make their own light, they couldn't rely on their sense of sight. They learned to use torches, oil lamps, and candles to light their way, but those things, having an open flame, gave off a lot of heat and just a little light.

These days we use electric bulbs, an invention less than a hundred years old. Inside the bulb there's a filament, a length of wire that's very thin. Electricity flows through it and makes it hot, but it doesn't catch fire as you would think it might: it gives off just a little heat and a lot of light.

At the end of our day, as the sun goes down and begins to fade, millions of incandescent bulbs come on, lighting up our homes and stores and streets to keep the dark at bay until we finally go to sleep. And only because of electric lights is it possible to work all night.

ARTIFICIAL LIGHT

WEIRTON STEEL WORKS, WEIRTON, WEST VIRGINIA

STEEL MILL

BLACKSMITH SHOP, FORT STEELE, BRITISH COLUMBIA

In the bronze age (twenty centuries past) people found certain rocks in the ground, and using fire to smelt them down, they made pure metal for swords and shields. We still make bronze, but now we also make iron and steel for everything from skyscrapers to automobiles. Iron softens at three thousand degrees, and once it's molten you can make it take any shape you please.

Sitting beside the railroad tracks, the steel mill is a place of dirty grays and sooty blacks, longer than four football fields. Inside, in a choking fog of sulfurous smoke, amidst the smell of iron and burning coke, as a cascade of sparks stab into the dark, with blinding orange light and chest-thumping roar, a gigantic ladle begins to pour its load of molten iron in a stream of liquid fire that will harden into steel.

STEEL MILL

OXYACETYLENE CUTTING TORCH

W E L D I N G

Some things just naturally burn very hot and fast. Acetylene is such a gas, and in the presence of oxygen it can burn very hot indeed, in the neighborhood of three thousand degrees. When the two gases together pass through the nozzle of a special torch, it can be used to easily cut a piece of steel in two. The flame it produces is so incredibly bright that unless you wear goggles it can damage your sight.

Yet another way that fire is used is to generate heat to melt the edges where two pieces of metal meet, so that when they're pressed together and cooled, it's as if they were a single piece—they're fused. That's called welding, and it's useful for making everything from airplanes to wedding rings.

FIREFIGHTERS, FREEPORT, NEW YORK

FIRE ON MAIN STREET

FIREFIGHTERS, FREEPORT, NEW YORK

Fire is useful in thousands of ways, it lights our nights and heats our days, but it's a terrible thing when it's out of control, taking lives and destroying homes. That's why at any time, in any weather, wherever people live together, whenever there's a fire, night or day, there are firefighters ready to fight the blaze.

FIRE ON MAIN STREET

CIVIL WAR ARTILLERY PIECE, GETTYSBURG, PENNSYLVANIA

FIREARMS

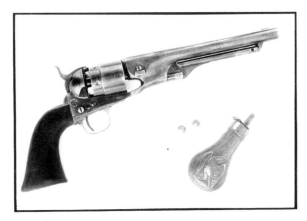

COLT REVOLVER AND POWDER FLASK

A thousand years ago or more, people invented a new tool for war. They discovered that certain substances explode when they burn, and when they do, they produce more than just light and heat: they release gases that expand with violent force. That force can drive a bullet at enormous speed from the barrel of a gun, or make a bomb to blow things up.

Firearms kill people and animals, too. That's essentially what they're meant to do. There was a time when we needed guns to hunt for food, but that's not so true anymore. Now most of us shop at the grocery store. It's true that many people use guns for harmless sport, but the largest number of guns are used for fighting wars. And perhaps it's a sign of the changing times, but more and more guns are used for committing crimes. The truth is—and it's sad to say—most guns are meant to kill people today.

LIFTOFF, SPACE SHUTTLE ATLANTIS

ROCKET LAUNCH

LIFTOFF, SPACE SHUTTLE COLUMBIA

When rocket fuel burns, it produces a huge volume of gas, which expands with colossal force and incredibly fast. In a rocket, because of the engine's shape, the gas has only one way to escape—it shoots out the back with a billow of flame, and a belching of smoke, and a wonderful, soul-shaking, thunderous roar. The rocket lifts off and commences to soar, to rise to the skies, from the surface of earth to the edges of space and beyond, to the moon and Mars, to the outer planets, and someday maybe even the stars.

ROCKET LAUNCH

LONE TRUCK, NEAR OMAHA, NEBRASKA

INTERNAL COMBUSTION

PUMPING GAS, EAST HAMPTON, NEW YORK

Inside the engine of a machine like a car, thousands of times in the course of a minute, a tiny bit of gasoline ignites, explodes, again and again, and the force of the explosions set in motion the moving parts of the working engine which, in turn, propels the car.

Internal combustion is what it's called, and it's changed the shape of the entire world. Everybody rushes around like fools, burning up our precious fuels at any cost, in cars, and trucks, and trains, and planes—and for all that speed, how much is gained and how much lost?

NEW YORK CITY SKYLINE

INCINERATOR

Sometimes we burn things to make them go away, like the garbage we sometimes incinerate. But one of the basic laws of nature essentially states that nothing disappears for real, it just changes form or shape. When you burn something, it doesn't really go away: part of it is turned to ash, the rest is turned to soot and gas. And we never quite know what shape it's in because it's chemically changed when it's burned: its molecules are rearranged—it may be poison, we often don't know. Part of it may remain in the air, the rest will settle down somewhere. We need to remember, whenever we can, to ask ourselves if that's quite fair.

INCINERATOR

FIRE-EATER

FIRE EATING

JUGGLING WITH FIRE

Playing with fire is a dangerous trick, that's part of what's so attractive about it. The fire-eater in the circus sticks a flaming torch inside his mouth and somehow puts the fire out. Of course, fire-eaters have to learn how to do that and not get burned. No one else should even try to do a trick that's played with fire.

FIRE EATING

MENORAH

<u>R I T U A L</u>

CIVIL WAR MEMORIAL, GETTYSBURG, PENNSYLVANIA

Long ago, at the end of the year when the days grew short, people feared that the sun might actually disappear. In modern times that notion seems odd, but the sun in those days was considered a god. So people lit bonfires, and sacrificial offerings were burned, in the hope that the full strength of the sun would return, and the crops would grow, and the people would thrive. Fire still has a place in our spiritual lives. Many cultures cremate their dead on funeral pyres, and some people imagine that sinners who die spend eternity roasting in fire. We light memorial candles to remember those who pass away, votive candles when we pray, and Sabbath candles on the seventh day. We light Christmas candles on Christmas night, and Chanukah is the Festival of Lights.

RITUAL

Acknowledgments
Thanks to David Weir, Mr. Charles Cronin of the Weirton Steel Company, Mr. Richard Hendrickson, Ira Bard, Mike Jody, Doug Kuntz, Gary Rieveschl, Hildy Maze, Genie Chipps, Lily Henderson, Randy Rosenthal, and special thanks to Ted Lawrence, the fire-eating circus guy.

Photo Credits:
All photographs by Ken Robbins except as noted below:
Volcano photograph on page 10 by Greg Vaughn.
Fire pictures on pages 34 and 35 by Ira Bard.
Shuttle launch photos on pages 38 and 39 courtesy of NASA.

All hand-coloring by Ken Robbins